WHAT IS OUT THERE?

by Dru Hunter

CREATIVE EDUCATION • CREATIVE PAPERBACKS

Published by **Creative Education** and **Creative Paperbacks**
P.O. Box 227, Mankato, Minnesota 56002
Creative Education and Creative Paperbacks are imprints of The Creative Company
www.thecreativecompany.us

Design and production by **Christine Vanderbeek**
Art direction by **Rita Marshall**
Printed in Malaysia

Photographs by Alamy (J Marshall-Tribaleye Images, The Natural History Museum,
PRISMA ARCHIVO), Corbis (145/Jeff Hunter/Ocean, Bettmann, Christie's Images,
CORBIS, Philippe Crassous/Science Photo Library, ALEXANDER DEMIANCHUK/
Reuters, Didier Dutheil/Sygma, DAVID GRAY/Reuters, Karen Kasmauski, Louie
Psihoyos, Roger Ressmeyer, Reuters, Michael T. Sedam, LOTHAR SLABON/epa,
Andrew Watson/JAI, Norbert Wu/Minden Pictures), Getty Images (Thomas J.
Abercrombie, Fred Bavendam/Minden Pictures, DEA PICTURE LIBRARY, Jeff Foott,
MARK GARLICK, Silvia Otte, Erik Simonsen, U.S. Navy/Handout, Bruno Vincent),
iStockphoto (imgendesign, Evgeny Terentev), NASA (Hinode JAXA/NASA/PPARC,
NASA/ESA/F. Paresce [INAF-IASF, Bologna, Italy]/ R. O'Connell [University of
Virginia, Charlottesville/Wide Field Camera 3 Science Oversight Committee),
Shutterstock (Steve Allen, Lee Prince, Alexander Raths, Marina Sun), Wikimedia
Commons (Steve Nicklas/NOS/NGS)

Library of Congress Cataloging-in-Publication Data
Hunter, Dru.
What is out there? / Dru Hunter.
p. cm. — (Think like a scientist)
Includes bibliographical references and index.
Summary: A narration of the origins, advancements, and future of the earth and space
sciences, including astronomy and geology, and the ways in which scientists utilize
the scientific method to explore questions.

ISBN 978-1-60818-594-8 (hardcover)
ISBN 978-1-62832-199-9 (pbk)

1. Earth sciences—Juvenile literature. 2. Space sciences—Juvenile literature. 3.
Scientists—Juvenile literature. 4. Science—Methodology—Juvenile literature. 5.
Science—History—Juvenile literature. I. Title.

QE29.H865 2015
550—dc23   2014030810

CCSS: RI.5.1, 2, 3, 8; RI.6.1, 3, 7; RST.6-8.1, 2, 5, 6, 8

First Edition HC 9 8 7 6 5 4 3 2 1
First Edition PBK 9 8 7 6 5 4 3 2 1

ON THE COVER Magnified close-up of mouthparts of a deep-
ocean worm found near hydrothermal vents

INTRODUCTION

Charles Wyville Thomson watched as sailors attached weights to the end of a rope. With a splash, the rope hit the water beside the HMS *Challenger*.

A former British wooden warship, the *Challenger* was now voyaging around the world on a scientific expedition supervised by the Scottish naturalist Thomson. The *Challenger* was making a sounding (measuring with a weighted line) to determine the ocean's depth at latitude 11°24′ north, longitude 143°16′ east, a location southwest of the Mariana Islands. At first, Thomson and his crew did not believe what they were seeing—their measurements were showing a depth of more than five miles (8 km)! Another sounding returned the same result. What they discovered would later be confirmed as the deepest point on Earth: 56 years after Thomson's voyage, *Challenger II* measured a depth of nearly 6.8 miles (10.9 km) at the spot that became known as the Challenger Deep.

Earth and space science is the study of our home planet and the celestial bodies around it. Earth scientists study the oceans (oceanographers), the land (geologists), and the **atmosphere** (meteorologists). Space scientists such as astronomers and astrophysicists study planets, moons, stars, and other topics related to outer space. Both earth and space scientists rely on other sciences, including physics, chemistry, and biology, to provide a basis for their studies. Using the **scientific method**, they look at how Earth and space operate and come up with theories and ways to test them. Their experiments lead to explanations as to how the earth and the universe got here in the first place.

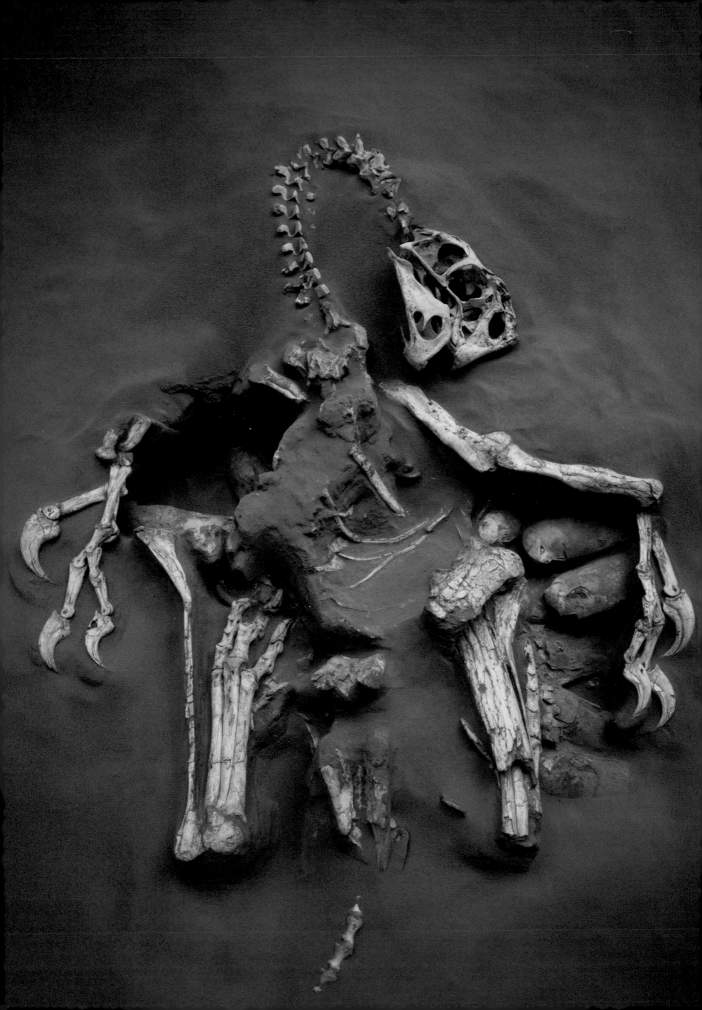

IN THE BEGINNING

G EOLOGY IS THE STUDY OF THE EARTH'S ROCKS AND formations. It involves how the land has been shaped and developed over time and includes the things, such as rocks, that are composed of one or more minerals. The ancient Greeks wrote about minerals and started to classify them by their hardness. Not until the 1600s did people become more interested in geology, though. At that time, a debate was raging among religious people over how to prove that the biblical Great Flood occurred. With more people digging for clues and exploring the different layers of the earth, it led to the discovery of **fossils** unlike any living creatures. The field of paleontology was born in the 1700s as people began studying prehistoric life.

The more people dug into the earth, the more useful things they found. Mining for energy sources and semi-precious metals made people rich and also provided

Fossils help scientists understand ancient creatures such as the birdlike Oviraptor.

resources such as coal and oil. During the 1800s, national governments began

to fund geological surveys to map areas where both mineral and non-mineral resources were located.

By the 1900s, scientists had developed radiometric dating. This method allowed scientists to determine a fossil's or mineral's age by measuring the amount of **radioactive decay** present. **Isotopes** within an element are either stable (such as what is found in nature) or unstable. Unstable isotopes give off energy in the form of radiation or radioactive decay. Radioactivity is measured by units called "curie," named after Marie and Pierre Curie, who discovered and worked with the element radium. The curie measures how many atoms decay per second. This technique could also date the age of the earth's rocks based on the radioactive isotopes inside them. The earth was estimated to be 4.6 billion years old.

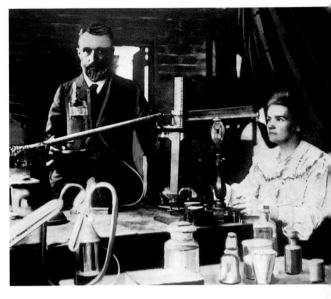

While some scientists study fault lines (opposite), the famed Curies (above) researched radioactivity.

In the 1960s, Harry Hess from Princeton University came up with the theory of seafloor spreading, which describes how the seafloor moves as it expands, carrying the continents with it. Hess's advancements in mapping the ocean's floors allowed scientists to prove the existence of plate tectonics. Earth's outermost layer is composed of several tectonic plates floating on the next layer. There are continental and oceanic plates. The plates move between 0.4 and 6.3 inches (1–16 cm) per year.

Where two plates meet is called a plate boundary. Typically, the plates either slide apart from or toward each other. These actions create events such as earthquakes. But they also cause geologic formations, such as mountains, to develop. Scientists estimate there are more than half a million earthquakes in the world every year. Most of the earthquakes are not severe enough to be felt, but about 100,000

JAMES HUTTON

James Hutton (1726–97) is called the "Father of Modern Geology." He was born in Scotland and studied chemistry and medicine at the universities of Edinburgh and Paris. After returning home to run his family's farm, he began to study the land. As he cleared away brush and dug drainage ditches, he observed that the rocks and layers of soil told a different story from what was taught at the time. In the 1700s, many people believed Earth was only 6,000 years old. Any fossils found were thought to belong to animals that had been killed during the biblical flood. Part of Hutton's evidence to the contrary was a cliff with layers of rock that he said proved the earth was composed of land and materials that had once been underwater—and it was constantly being re-formed. Hutton's methods of studying the earth made geology a science.

are noticed—and 100 of these do actual damage. The two deadli-
est earthquakes on record have both occurred in China because it is
squeezed between the Pacific, Indian, and Philippine plates. When
one plate shifts, it oftentimes has a violent effect on the country's
dense population. In 1556, an earthquake struck central China and
killed an estimated 800,000 people. In 1976, an earthquake killed
more than 242,000 in Tangshan, China.

Seismologists are scientists who study earthquakes.
They use two rating systems to measure the magnitude
of, or energy released by, earthquakes. In 1935, American
seismologist Charles Richter developed what became
known as the Richter scale. It was replaced in the 1970s
by the moment magnitude scale (MMS). Seismologists
Thomas Hanks and Hiroo Kanamori introduced the
MMS because some earthquakes at the time exceeded
the Richter scale. The MMS uses the values of 1 to 10 to
express the size of a quake and is denoted by the letter
M. The other earthquake rating scientists assign is the
Mercalli rating. Mercalli measures an earthquake's intensi-

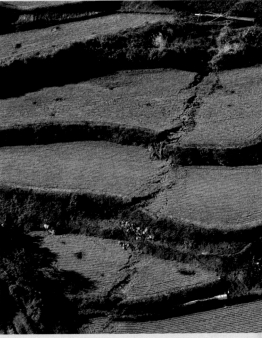

*Japan's Nojima fault trig-
gered the 1995 Great Han-
shin earthquake, which killed
more than 6,000 people.*

ty. A degree I earthquake on the Mercalli scale means it was not felt
by most people, while degree XII is when everything is destroyed, as
in the catastrophic 1920 Haiyuan earthquake in China.

Underwater earthquakes create tsunamis, which are giant sea
waves. A 9.0 M earthquake off the east coast of Japan in 2011 created waves up to 133 feet (40.5 m) high. The tsunami drowned towns
along Japan's coast and caused nearly 16,000 deaths.

Seismic activity is not limited to Earth. When astronauts first
visited the moon in 1969, they placed seismometers on the surface
to measure the moon's quakes and send the data back to scientists on Earth. Additional moonquake seismometers were placed

DID YOU KNOW? The precious stones rubies, sapphires, and emeralds are rarer than diamonds. Other diamond colors besides white are yellow, blue, and green—but the rarest is red (shown above).

on the moon through 1972. They were able to record thousands of moonquakes. What scientists at the National Aeronautics and Space Administration (NASA) found was that moonquakes seem to take four forms. The majority of moonquakes occur deep inside the moon—more than 435 miles (700 km) below the surface. Moonquakes are ranked below a magnitude of 3 on the Richter scale. However, they can last for 10 minutes or longer. There is evidence that deep moonquakes are caused by the gravitational pull Earth has on the moon during the tides. Moonquakes can also occur at shallow depths and sometimes result after a **meteorite** strikes the surface. A fourth type, known as the thermal moonquake, happens when the moon's surface is exposed to sunlight after two weeks of freezing nights.

Other aspects of the moon and outer space fall under the scope of astronomers. Astronomy is an old science. The ancient Egyptians studied astronomy and built monuments such as the pyramids at Giza to align with certain stars. The Great Pyramid of Khufu was aligned true north to point toward the North Star, Polaris. Some Egyptian temples were designed to allow sunlight to come inside only once per year. Other Egyptian temples recorded the phases of the moon. What is known about ancient Egyptian astronomy comes from paintings found inside tombs, inscriptions on the walls and columns of temples, and writings on papyrus scrolls.

It was the invention of the refracting telescope in 1608 by Dutch eyeglass maker Hans Lippershey that spurred astronomy's growth as a science. Lippershey made his telescope to see objects far away. He used lenses to make the viewed image appear upright, and the telescope had a three-times magnification. The next year, Italian physicist and astronomer Galileo Galilei made a more powerful telescope and discovered the four largest moons of Jupiter in 1610.

Modern telescopes such as the Hubble Space Telescope have a clearer view of space than telescopes on Earth because they are free of Earth's atmosphere.

Many aspects of black holes remain a mystery to humans, spurring speculations of future time travel.

Based on images collected from Hubble since 1990, astronomers **hypothesize** the universe is about 13 to 14 billion years old. Astronomers use physics and computers to explain what they observe in space. Hubble images have helped astronomers locate black holes, points in space where the pull of gravity is so strong that it does not allow even light to escape. Hubble has also assisted scientists in hypothesizing on the existence of dark energy, a force estimated to fill 68.3 percent of the universe and to cause the universe to expand at a faster rate. The important space telescope has also provided scientists with more information about what happens when stars die.

In late 2013, planetary scientists used Hubble to detect water in the atmospheres of five planets beyond our solar system. Scientists do not think these exoplanets have life on them—at least, not life as we know it—but the "hot Jupiters" will be studied nonetheless.

TRY IT OUT! Too much carbon, nitrogen, and sulfur dioxide in the atmosphere makes **acid rain**, which erodes rocks. To see erosion in action, place a piece of limestone in a glass, and pour some vinegar over it. Observe the bubbles. The vinegar is eating away at the rock!

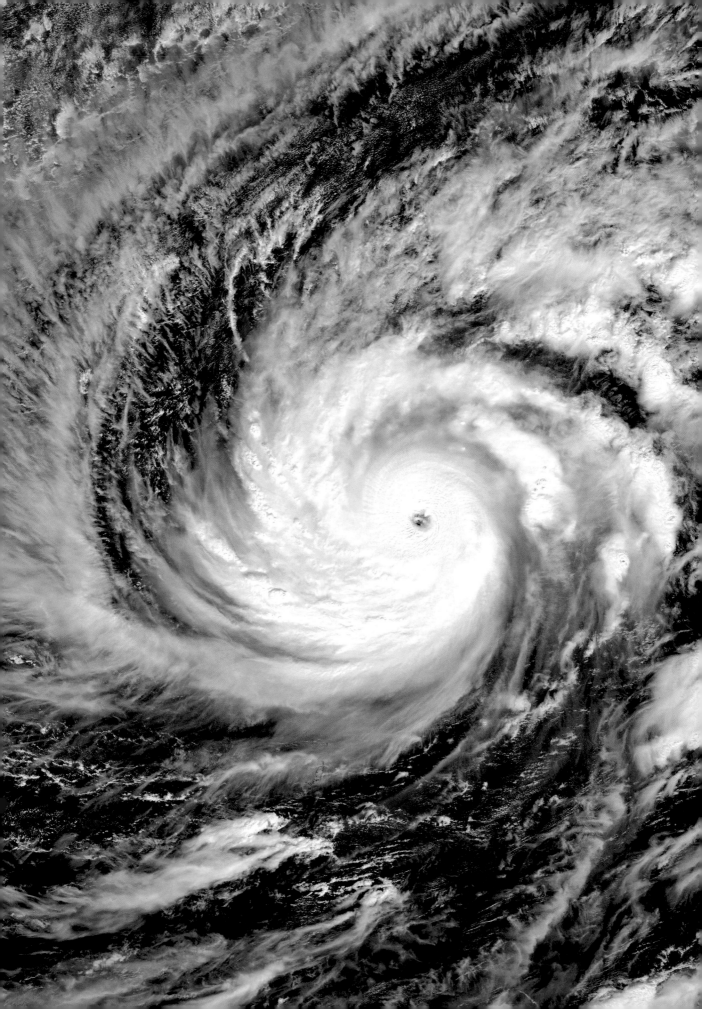

WATER WORLD

L IQUID WATER COVERS 71 PERCENT OF OUR PLANET and supports all known kinds of life. Earth keeps its water in a constant cycle, which makes the planet habitable. Surface water evaporates into the air and forms clouds. When the clouds become heavy with moisture, the water returns to Earth as **precipitation**. Earth scientists who study this ongoing water cycle are called hydrologists.

On January 23, 1960, Swiss oceanographer Jacques Piccard and American naval lieutenant Don Walsh descended to the deepest part of the ocean, the Challenger Deep, in a bathyscaphe called *Trieste*. Designed by Piccard and his father, the submersible vehicle was built for researching and observing record ocean depths. An external tank filled with 34,000 gallons (128,704 l) of gasoline was employed to make *Trieste* ascend after its record-breaking dive was complete.

Spiraling high winds form the calm center of a hurricane, known as the eye.

It took *Trieste* nearly five hours to get the two men to the bottom of the

Challenger Deep. During the descent, a window in the entrance tunnel to the bathyscaphe had cracked, and the men wanted to surface while there would still be daylight remaining, in case any emergencies occurred. For 20 minutes, though, Piccard and Walsh made as many scientific observations and recorded as many instrument readings as possible.

The interior of Trieste's pressurized sphere gave Piccard and Walsh only 7.1 feet (2.2 m) of space.

They could see sand-colored ooze made up of the remains of microscopic algae. Near the ocean bottom, Piccard thought he saw very small jellyfish. The pressure at that depth was 16,000 pounds per square inch (1,125kg/cm²)— equal to 32,000 cars stacked on top of a person's chest. The thermometer registered 37.4 °F (3 °C) in areas farther from hydrothermal vents (where temperatures can climb to 572 °F, or 300 °C). Other expeditions in the 1990s and 2012 involved both manned and unmanned vessels exploring the Mariana Trench. At approximately 180 million years of age, the Mariana Trench's seabed is one of the oldest on Earth, and scientists have discovered more than 200 different organisms from mud samples in the Challenger Deep. Among them are translucent animals resembling sea cucumbers, shrimp-like creatures, and snails with soft shells. Bacteria thrive around hydrothermal vents. Higher up the trench, yet still at depths of about 20,000 feet (6,096 m), white clams have been found as well as deep-ocean organisms such as comb jellies and eels. There, deeper-dwelling creatures live longer than those at shallower depths—perhaps because there are fewer predators. Researchers can estimate the age of such Mariana Trench life forms as clams by counting lines on their shells. Many deep-sea creatures live longer than 100 years.

The longest chain of mountains on Earth is beneath the ocean. In the 1950s, scientists mapped the midocean ridge with sonar.

ALFRED WEGENER

Alfred Wegener (1880–1930) was born in Germany and earned a doctorate in astronomy. Pursuing an interest in the new science of meteorology, Wegener and his brother then pioneered the use of weather balloons (shown above). In 1906, they set a record for balloon flight by flying for 52.5 hours. Later that year, Wegener built the first weather station on Greenland. He thought about why fossils and similar species unable to swim oceans were found on different continents. In 1912, Wegener proposed his continental drift theory that the continents used to be one landmass called "Urkontinent" (later named Pangaea). He used geologic evidence from rocks and fossils on both sides of the Atlantic Ocean to try to prove his point and noted that, if the ocean between Africa and South America were removed, those continents would fit together perfectly. The theory continued to be criticized until more proof

Sonar is a system that detects underwater objects by making sound waves and measuring the time it takes for the sound to bounce back. Oceanographers have determined that midocean ridges cover more than 31,000 miles (49,890 km) and encircle the seafloor like the seams of a softball.

Geologist Harry Hess studied the maps of the midocean ridges and began to ask questions about what he was seeing. In 1960, he considered whether what he was observing could prove the 1912 theory of continental drift proposed by geophysicist Alfred Wegener. Hess proposed his own theory of seafloor spreading to support the hypothesis behind continental drift. The new theory provided an explanation for the movement of continents (because motion in the seafloor would carry continents with it).

Hess described the concept in terms similar to the workings of conveyer belts, explaining how the ocean floors shifted the conti-nents when they moved. His studies of the midocean ridges showed that volcanic activity caused **magma** to surface along cracks in the ridges, pushing the older rock farther away on either side of the ridge. The freshly surfaced hot rock then cooled and formed new crust on the seafloor, thus spreading.

Some of the scientific evidence that added proof of seafloor spreading was collected by the *Glomar Challenger*, a deep-sea drilling vessel, in 1968 and the submersible *Alvin* later in 1974. The *Glomar Challenger* drilled core samples from the deep-ocean seafloors between South America and Africa over a period of 15 years. By determining the age of the samples through radiometric dating, scientists gained additional proof of both the seafloor and plate tectonic theories. Built to withstand the crushing pressure of the ocean at a depth of 14,800 feet (4,511 m), *Alvin* was able to dive

The Glomar Challenger *confirmed plate tectonics by finding the ocean floor to be much younger than Earth.*

DID YOU KNOW? About 90 percent of Earth's volcanic activity occurs in the ocean; Mauna Loa (shown in background) in Hawaii is the largest active volcano.

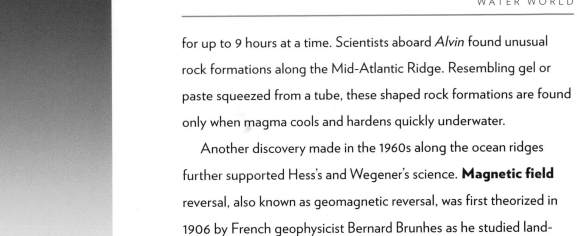

for up to 9 hours at a time. Scientists aboard *Alvin* found unusual rock formations along the Mid-Atlantic Ridge. Resembling gel or paste squeezed from a tube, these shaped rock formations are found only when magma cools and hardens quickly underwater.

Another discovery made in the 1960s along the ocean ridges further supported Hess's and Wegener's science. **Magnetic field** reversal, also known as geomagnetic reversal, was first theorized in 1906 by French geophysicist Bernard Brunhes as he studied land-based volcanic eruptions. The earth has a magnetic field around its core that protects the planet from harmful particles such as the sun's radiation and solar winds.

As Brunhes researched the rocks produced by an ancient lava flow, he noticed that they were magnetized in the opposite direction from where they should have been. He knew that iron produced by cooling magma is attracted to the magnetic North Pole. But these rocks seemed to be magnetized to the South Pole. The iron inside the cooling lava aligned with the direction of Earth's magnetic field similar to a compass. Brunhes hypothesized that, at some point in the past, Earth's magnetic field had been reversed. Scientists such as British marine geologists Fred Vine and Drummond Matthews discovered rocks on the ocean floor that also showed records of such reversals. It took 50 years after Brunhes made his discovery for it to be accepted, thanks to additional proof provided by Vine and others. Scientists have now shown that Earth's magnetic field has reversed about 60 times in the past 20 million years.

The scientists who really dig into the ancient history of life on Earth are paleontologists. Sankar Chatterjee, curator of paleontology at the Museum of Texas Tech University, believes that life began in the deep sea 4 billion years ago. This early ocean had an abundance of life, and some of it still exists today. Growing to

17 feet (5.2 m) wide, with a 10-inch (25.4 cm) poisonous, dagger-like tail, the giant stingray swims in murky rivers in Australia. Stingrays survived in the water for millions of years while dinosaurs walked the land. Excavations on the Isle of Skye have found fossil evidence that turtles were swimming 164 million years ago during the time of the dinosaurs as well. Dinosaurs ate turtles and their eggs. The dinosaurs went extinct about 65 million years ago, but animals—such as sturgeon and lungfish—that are still here today in much the same form as they were back then are called "living fossils."

The gigantic-jawed Megalodon (opposite) was outlived by the much smaller but adaptable sturgeon (above).

Studying more than 400 fossilized teeth of *Megalodon*, a shark almost as large as an 18-wheeler truck, helped Catalina Pimiento and her colleagues from the paleontology division of the Florida Museum of Natural History discover a possible 10-million-year-old shark nursery in Panama. Based on the fossil record, *Megalodon* lived from about 28 to 1.5 million years ago. It is said to have looked like a massive great white shark and hunted whales. Paleontologists hypothesize *Megalodon* went extinct because of cooler ocean temperatures and a decline in its food supply.

TRY IT OUT! Find Africa on a globe or map. Using a sheet of paper and pencil, trace the continent's west coast. Next, find the east coast of South America, and line up your trace of Africa. See how they fit!

SCIENTISTS IN ACTION

EARTH SCIENTISTS SUCH AS PALEONTOLOGIST PAUL Sereno travel around the world to make discoveries about the earth today. "That is part of the fun and excitement of science," he has said. "You never know where it is going to take you." Sereno's first adventure in 1988 took him to the foothills of the Andes Mountains in Argentina. In an area known as the Valley of the Moon, he and his team discovered fossils from dinosaurs that lived 230 million years ago during the Late Triassic period.

For a living organism to fossilize, it has to be preserved in excellent condition. Fossilization is the process by which an organism's remains are replaced or cast in rock. Digging out fossils is meticulous work. Using tools such as paintbrushes and tiny picks, paleontologists gently brush away the dirt and remove debris from around a fossil.

In 1997, Sereno (left) and his team dug up 95 percent of the long-necked Jobaria.

The dinosaurs Dr. Sereno and his colleagues discovered in the Valley

the Moon were some of the first to roam the earth. One specimen, *Eodromaeus* (meaning "dawn runner"), likely weighed about 11 pounds (5 kg) and had a long neck and tail. "It really is the earliest look we have at the long line of meat eaters that would ultimately culminate in *Tyrannosaurus rex* near the end of the dinosaur era," said Dr. Sereno.

Another fossil-hunting expedition took Dr. Sereno and his team to Africa. There they excavated more than 70 tons (63.5 t) from the rocks and sand of the Sahara Desert. Some of the fossils dated back 110 to 112 million years, including those of an early relative of the crocodile, *Sarcosuchus imperator.* Nicknamed "SuperCroc," it weighed as much as an elephant—8.8 tons (8 t)—and grew as long as a school bus, equal to about 40 feet (12.2 m). Although fossils from earlier findings had offered small pieces of information on the crocodilian, scientists did not have a complete picture of its enormous size until Sereno and his team made their discoveries.

In all, Sereno found six specimens of the SuperCroc—one had enough of the skeleton intact that scientists were able to theorize about its appearance. The jaws alone were six feet (1.8 m) tall. The more than 100 teeth were hypothesized to have torn into the flesh of unsuspecting prey. "We had never seen anything like it," Dr. Sereno said. "The snout and teeth were designed for grabbing prey—fish, turtles, and dinosaurs that strayed too close." From fossilized scutes (bony plates), paleontologists were able to estimate SuperCroc's age. Similar to the way tree rings form in a trunk as a tree grows, SuperCroc's scutes showed evidence of annual growing circles. These told the scientists that SuperCroc could live to about age 60.

For paleontologists such as Sereno, the thrill of scientific

The Valley of the Moon (opposite) attracts fossil hunters eager for finds as exciting as SuperCroc (below).

SCIENTIST IN THE SPOTLIGHT

MARY ANNING

Mary Anning (1799–1847) was born in Lyme Regis, a town on the southern coast of England. Of 10 children, only Mary and her brother Joseph survived. When Mary was 12, she and Joseph found a skeleton of what would become the first identified ichthyosaur. The cliffs near the seashore where the Annings lived were abundant in fossils, and Mary knew how to find them. Over several months in 1811, she carefully excavated a nearly complete prehistoric crocodile skeleton. This was sold to a museum in London and brought her to the attention of scientists as a fossil hunter. She made many more fossil discoveries, including the first plesiosaur skeleton. Mary taught herself geology, and prominent scientists of her time came to her fossil shop, often purchasing specimens (such as *Rhomaleosaurus cramptoni*, pictured above) for their collections. Grateful for her help, geologist Louis Agassiz even named two fossilized fish species after Anning.

discovery keeps them digging for more. "I see paleontology as adventure with a purpose," Dr. Sereno said. "How else to describe a science that allows you to romp in remote corners of the globe, resurrecting gargantuan creatures that have never been seen? And the trick to big fossil finds? You've got to be able to go where no one has gone before."

Oceanographer Sylvia Earle has gone many places in our oceans where no one else has gone before. When Earle was a college student at Florida State University, she learned how to scuba dive and has since dived in more than 6,000 research and experimental dives. She has led more than 100 oceanic expeditions. One of the first female aquanauts on the planet, she led a Tektite II mission in 1970, spending two weeks in an underwater lab off the coast of the U.S. Virgin Islands. She set a record for the deepest untethered dive by a woman in 1979, diving to 1,250 feet (381 m) off the coast of Hawaii. A submersible carried her down, and she released the tether connecting them. Wearing a bulky, pressurized JIM suit, which resembles what the Apollo astronauts wore on the moon, Earle was able to explore the seafloor for two hours. In 1986, she set the record for a woman's deepest solo dive (and tied the overall record) when she dove to 3,280 feet (1,000 m) in the sub *Deep Rover*.

Besides spending more than 7,000 hours underwater, Earle worked with deep-sea robots from inside ships.

From 1990 to 1992, Dr. Earle served as the first female chief scientist at the National Oceanic and Atmospheric Administration (NOAA). The agency performs underwater research, manages fisheries, and oversees marine environmental disasters. Earle became an expert on the impact of oil spills on marine life and was one of the first scientists to dive into the Persian Gulf after Iraqi troops set fire to oil fields in Kuwait.

DID YOU KNOW? *Tyrannosaurus rex* had about 60 teeth, each tooth 10 inches (25.4 cm) long, and it could tear off a 500-pound (227 kg) piece of meat in a single chomp.

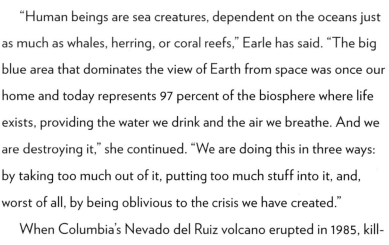

"Human beings are sea creatures, dependent on the oceans just as much as whales, herring, or coral reefs," Earle has said. "The big blue area that dominates the view of Earth from space was once our home and today represents 97 percent of the biosphere where life exists, providing the water we drink and the air we breathe. And we are destroying it," she continued. "We are doing this in three ways: by taking too much out of it, putting too much stuff into it, and, worst of all, by being oblivious to the crisis we have created."

When Columbia's Nevado del Ruiz volcano erupted in 1985, killing more than 23,000 people, the U.S. Geological Survey implemented a program to help other countries get through a volcano crisis. Volcanologist Dan Miller has said when a volcano starts to show unrest, "we select a team of scientists with the kind of expertise that is requested and required, and we take the kinds of equipment with us that will help out." He explained they bring three tools to predict eruptions, including "a telemetered volcanic seismic monitoring network to detect the earthquakes that often precede eruptions. Second, tiltmeters and electronic distance measuring equipment to monitor bulging or deformation that results from magma pushing up against the solid rock of the volcano. Finally, devices to measure sulfur dioxide and carbon dioxide."

William Sager, volcanologist at the University of Houston, uncovered in 2013 the largest volcano on Earth. Located underwater around 1,000 miles (1,609 km) from Japan, Tamu Massif is about the size of New Mexico and almost as large as some of the massive volcanoes on the planet Mars, making it one of the biggest in this solar system. Sager has been studying Tamu Massif for 20 years, and, until core sample data could be collected from the *JOIDES Resolution* research vessel, he wasn't sure if it was one volcano or several. According to Sager, "Tamu Massif is the biggest single

shield volcano ever discovered on Earth." The volcano covers approximately 120,000 square miles (310,799 sq km). In comparison, Mauna Loa in Hawaii—Earth's biggest active volcano—is about 2,000 square miles (5,180 sq km).

Sager has said Tamu Massif is around 145 million years old and the top of it is roughly 6,500 feet (1,981 m). The bottom of the volcano is four miles (6.4 km) deep in the ocean, which is one of the many obstacles in studying it. "An immense amount of magma came from the center, and this magma had to have come from the earth's mantle," Sager has explained. "So this is important information for geologists trying to understand how the earth's interior works."

In 2009, an undersea volcano near Tonga erupted, spouting ash, smoke, and steam over the Pacific.

TRY IT OUT! To find out what it is like to be a paleontologist trying to dig out a fossil from a rock without damaging it, try to dig out a chocolate chip from a cookie using a toothpick!

FUTURE EARTH

ONE OF THE MOST PRESSING ISSUES FACING TODAY'S oceanographers is ocean acidification. To get an idea of what Earth would look like if ocean acidity continues to rise, scientists have set up experiments in labs and in the ocean. They are conducting tests and recording results that show how organisms are adapting to different acidic levels. Another approach some scientists are taking involves researching the fossil records. These scientists look back in Earth's history to a time when ocean acidity matched the level they estimate we will see in the near future.

Around 55 million years ago, an increase in volcanic activity produced high levels of carbon dioxide. When the oceans absorbed that gas, the water became more acidic. The oceans during this time were not able to sustain many coral reefs, oxygen levels were poor, food chains were affected, and large deep-sea predators such as prehistoric sharks faced extinction. In 2013, scientists from Germany's Alfred

From brown algae to fish, Earth's oceans and seas support a variety of life.

Wegener Institute used ocean field tests and the fossil records to show that such acidification has a negative effect on marine life.

Half of the living coral in Australia's Great Barrier Reef has died in the last 30 years because of cyclones, rising ocean temperatures, and the predatory behavior of crown-of-thorns starfish—each of which can consume 12 square yards (10 sq m) of coral annually. Scientists hypothesize that rising ocean acidity levels will further stress reefs across the globe, and human contributions to that acidity are speeding up the process. Activities such as pollution and overfishing lead to other problems in the oceans as well.

Although the fossil record has shown that, over time, sea creatures can adapt to changing conditions, fish are still sensitive to variations in acidity. Scientists today are trying to find out if species will be able to adapt quickly enough, since the acidic changes fish experienced in the past were not as rapid as they are now. The National Research Council's Ocean Studies Board noted in a 2013 report that oceanic acidity could increase by as much as 150 percent by the year 2100, if emissions are not controlled. Scientists look for answers to questions about reducing carbon emissions and wonder what it will mean to Earth's land, oceans, and living things if solutions are not found in the near future.

The Great Barrier Reef (opposite) contains hundreds of types of coral (above) that help maintain the ecosystem.

Scientists say we still know very little about Earth's oceans, and it is difficult to predict what the future will bring. Although we have accurate maps of Earth's land features—and area maps of the moon—less than 10 percent of the seafloor has been recorded. Twelve men have walked on the moon, while only three men have been to the bottom of the ocean. Scientists have accounted for about 250,000 species at home in our planet's waters, and they estimate there may

EDWIN HUBBLE

Edwin Hubble (1889–1953) grew up reading science fiction by Jules Verne and other authors. While at the University of Chicago, he studied math and astronomy and worked as assistant to Dr. Robert Millikan, who would later win the Nobel Prize for Physics in 1923. Hubble became a lawyer before he returned to school for a doctorate in astronomy. He put his knowledge to work at the Mount Wilson Observatory in California and was able to use the Hooker telescope to prove that other galaxies existed beyond our Milky Way. With the help of assistant Milton Humason, Hubble came up with the concept known as Hubble's law to explain how the universe was expanding. This theory also gave astronomers the means of calculating the approximate age of the universe. When NASA was developing a space telescope in the 1980s, they named it after astronomy's brightest star, Edwin Hubble (shown at left with the Schmidt Photographic Telescope).

be millions more yet to be discovered. After all, one of the largest animals in the ocean, the giant squid, was not seen alive in the deep ocean until recently.

The ocean supplies more than half the oxygen we breathe. It affects both long-term and short-term weather patterns and events. Some people think the ocean cannot be harmed because it is so vast and deep. However, science has shown that we can hurt the ocean when we pollute it with any type of waste. We can also cause damage when we remove materials from it through activities such as drilling and fishing. The more knowledge we gather about our oceans and the formations above and below them, the more we are able to apply information to the study of the universe as a whole.

Hawking wrote his popular books to help non-specialists understand scientific concepts and theories.

Theoretical physicist and cosmologist Stephen Hawking uses physics and math to research the universe. From an early age, he was curious about how the world around him worked. When he was 21, as a physics major and a member of Oxford University's rowing team, he found out he had Lou Gehrig's disease, a neurological disorder that makes him lose control of his muscles. Told he had only a few years to live, Hawking was driven to find purpose in his family and in studying the universe. One of his great achievements was to co-develop with Jim Hartle the 1983 theory that the universe has no boundary. Famous for his work related to black holes and his book *A Brief History of Time*, Hawking became convinced that humans should explore space **colonization**. With the threats posed to our planet—from global warming to nuclear warfare—Hawking expressed in 2012 that "we will eventually establish self-sustaining colonies on Mars and other bodies in the solar system, although probably not within the next 100 years." He continued, "I am optimistic that progress in science and

DID YOU KNOW? It is estimated that every second, the sun's core releases bursts of energy that are equivalent to 100 billion nuclear bombs.

technology will eventually enable humans to spread beyond the solar system and out into the far reaches of the universe."

Before we get to that point, though, there is still much to learn about the universe. Some of the data retrieved from the most powerful telescopes baffles astronomers. Physics as we know it does not always account for some of the occurrences space scientists observe. In an effort to take space study even deeper than the Hubble Space Telescope has allowed, NASA is collaborating with Canadian and European space agencies to develop the James Webb Space Telescope (JWST). The project is set to launch in 2018. Unlike Hubble, which was placed into Earth **orbit** by a space shuttle, the JWST will be launched by a rocket from the European Spaceport near Kourou, French Guiana.

The new infrared telescope is expected to help space scientists unravel what happened after the Big Bang, a point in time nearly 14 billion years ago when many scientists believe the universe grew from being smaller than a single atom to the size of a galaxy. The JWST will allow scientists to study stars that are similar to our sun while they are young, giving us a glimpse into how our own solar system may have formed. And the new instrument will continue combing the galaxies for other solar systems and planets. In the process, the JWST should help us learn more about our own.

Closer to Earth are thousands of satellites that already monitor or communicate with systems on the ground. NASA has more than a dozen earth science satellites studying the atmosphere, land, and ocean. They can track ice sheets and measure the volume of gases, such as carbon dioxide, present in the atmosphere. During natural disasters, satellites also measure volcanic ash and smoke. A lot of satellites fall out of orbit when they stop working and burn up in the atmosphere before they can reach the earth. Some satellites

continue to orbit, even when no longer operational, and are considered space junk. Scientists are working on building longer-lasting satellites for the future that can move themselves to lower orbits, gradually reentering the atmosphere to dispose of themselves.

Earth scientists are also continuing to improve natural disaster warning systems to alert people with as much time as possible before a tsunami, hurricane, earthquake, or volcano eruption. But after a meteor measuring 55 feet (16.8 m) exploded over Russia in February 2013, people were reminded that there exist other threats in our active universe. Together, earth and space scientists monitor and work to understand our planet and all that lies beyond.

Weather satellites (opposite) provide climate data, while GPS satellites (above) give location and time.

TRY IT OUT! To find Polaris, the North Star, first use a compass to find north. From the horizon, look up about a third of the distance to the sky. It may not be a **first magnitude** star, but the North Star is bright!

acid rain: rain with high sulfur and nitrogen content that harms the environment; often caused by the burning of fossil fuels

atmosphere: a mass of gases that surrounds Earth or another planet

colonization: the act of sending settlers to an area to live

first magnitude: describing stars that are the brightest in the sky

fossils: the remains of ancient creatures, sometimes found changed into a stony substance or as a mold impressed into rock

hypothesize: to make an educated guess; to suggest an explanation based on a limited amount of evidence

isotopes: atoms within an element that have equal numbers of protons and electrons but a different amount of neutrons

magma: liquid rock beneath the earth's crust that sometimes can contain fragments of rock, dissolved gases, and crystals

magnetic field: surrounding lines of force from a fixed magnetic object that acts on other magnets

meteorite: an outer space rock or metal object that is the remains of a meteor after landing on Earth

orbit: the curved path revolving around an object in space

precipitation: rain, sleet, snow, or any kind of weather condition that falls from the sky

radioactive decay: energy in the form of radiation emitted by elements with unstable isotopes; also known as radioactivity

scientific method: a step-by-step method of research that includes making observations, forming hypotheses, performing experiments, and analyzing results

shield volcano: a low-lying volcano built from lava that erupts in all directions, forming a sheet of fluid lava

Corfield, Richard. *The Silent Landscape: The Scientific Voyage of HMS* Challenger. Washington, D.C.: Joseph Henry, 2003.

Denny, Mark. *How the Ocean Works: An Introduction to Oceanography*. Princeton, N.J.: Princeton University Press, 2008.

Larsen, Kristine. *Stephen Hawking: A Biography*. Amherst, N.Y.: Prometheus, 2007.

Liu, Charles. *The Handy Astronomy Answer Book*. Canton, Mich.: Visible Ink, 2008.

Oldroyd, David. *Earth Cycles: A Historical Perspective*. Westport, Conn.: Greenwood, 2006.

Skinner, Brian J., and Stephen C. Porter. *The Dynamic Earth: An Introduction to Physical Geology*. 4th ed. New York: Wiley, 2000.

Sverdrup, Keith A., Alyn C. Duxbury, and Alison B. Duxbury. *An Introduction to the World's Oceans*. 7th ed. Boston: McGraw-Hill, 2003.

Zimmerman, Robert. *The Universe in a Mirror: The Saga of the Hubble Telescope and the Visionaries Who Built It*. Princeton, N.J.: Princeton University Press, 2008.

READY: KNOW THE FACTS
http://www.ready.gov/kids/know-the-facts
This website gives information and safety tips about different natural disasters such as tsunamis and earthquakes.

WINDOWS TO THE UNIVERSE: KIDS' SPACE
http://www.windows2universe.org/kids_space/kids_space.html
Play games and do activities that cover topics from the carbon cycle to space junk.

Note: Every effort has been made to ensure that the websites listed above are suitable for children, that they have educational value, and that they contain no inappropriate material. However, because of the nature of the Internet, it is impossible to guarantee that these sites will remain active indefinitely or that their contents will not be altered.